FOR MY DAUGHTER, WITH LOVE

Written by: Ken Hedrington

Illustrated by: Meredith Lucius

Written by Ken Hedrington
Illustrated by Meredith Lucius
Book Design by Amanda Mishelle
Published by For Her Press
Roswell, Georgia
hello@kenhedrington.com

Printed in the United States of America
ISBN: 979-8-9993351-0-4

To my wife, who made me a husband, and then a dad.
And to my daughter, who made me realize I'm not actually in charge of anything around here.

To the little girl I have just met
You are already making me into
The father I want to be

I don't know what you will love
Or what you will grow up to be
But by your side I hope to always be

Through heartbreak and triumph
The ups and the downs
As long as you'll have me
I would love to be around

The thought of your laughs and even your many firsts
Remind me that the little girl I have just met
Will soon be the little girl I will never forget

You will know that you are loved
And that love will not be up for debate
To know your worth is the first lesson I hope you will take

Fail early and often is what my dad always said
I often sit back and wonder what world awaits you ahead

I can't promise you I will be perfect
But I will promise to be kind
I just hope that you will be patient
with me, this is my first time

You remind me so much of your mother
Which is so beautiful to me
Your face will be a constant reminder
Of how our love brought you to me

No matter how old you are my love has no expiration date
You will always be daddy's little girl regardless of what you say

No matter the place, no matter the time
I will show up when you need me every single time

When it's all said and done
And we both look back on our days
My hope is that you'll remember me
As a girl dad, your dad
For the rest of your days

DEAR GIRL DAD,

I couldn't leave out my guys!
Being a girl dad is one of the greatest titles you'll ever carry.
It's not about being perfect — it's about being present.
It's about wiping away tears, celebrating every win, and being her safe
place when the world feels too big.
You won't always get it right (none of us do), but your love will always
matter. She'll remember the way you made her feel — strong, worthy, and
deeply loved.
You're her first hero. Her forever home.
Walk proud, love big, and enjoy every second — even the crazy ones.

From one girl dad to another,
Ken Hedrington

DAD, DRAW YOUR DAUGHTER HERE!

DAUGHTER, DRAW YOUR DAD HERE!

FOR MY DAUGHTER, WITH LOVE

A special message from a Dad to his daughter.

THANK YOU

Thank you for reading For My Daughter, With Love.
This book was created for the quiet moments, the deep bonds, and the love
that lives between a father and his daughter.

To all the dads who took time to read, reflect, and connect —
and to all the daughters who will carry those words in their hearts —
I hope this story becomes a memory you both cherish.

Here's to the love that lasts a lifetime,
and the stories we pass from one generation to the next.

With gratitude,

www.ingramcontent.com/pod-product-compliance
Lightning Source LLC
Chambersburg PA
CBHW041621120626
46551CB00003B/530